A CREATOR'S COMPANION

A HANDBOOK FOR THE PRACTICE OF CREATION

LIAM BOWLER

© 2021 by Liam Bowler
All rights reserved
First edition
Printed in the United States of America

Editor: Jennifer Sanders
Art: Meg Yates
Design: Danny Schmidt

ISBN: 978-1-7365433-2-0

LAND ACKNOWLEDGEMENT

This book was written on the land of the Pacific Northwest, near where the Nooksack River meets the sea. Thank you to the life here in its many forms — the slugs, cedars, stones, hawks, mycelium, and giant firs — who are in this book as much as what I've ever learned in a class.

I want to acknowledge the people who have stewarded this land since long before the arrival of white settlers: the Coast Salish people, particularly the Lummi Nation and the Nooksack Tribe. Much of this land was taken violently from these tribes — a truth I was largely shielded from viscerally experiencing as a child in school. May we tell the story as it is, and honor the wisdom that is alive in these and other indigenous cultures, not only because it is kind and sane to turn back towards someone you've wounded and say "I'm sorry; how can I help make this right?" but also because we are in desperate need of different frameworks about who we are, and what the world is, in this time of great social and ecological crisis.

For my dad, Printer.

Everything in creation
is intended to relieve a need.
Everything that grows,
grows because someone, somewhere,
awaits it.

— Rumi

TABLE OF CONTENTS

Foreword
Preface
How to Use This Book

OPENING 1

    The Call 2
    A Walk in the Woods 3
    Who This Book Is For 5
    On Writing 6
    On Method 7
    Creation's Process 8
    Creating as a Practice 9
    Surfing 10
    Roses 11
    Why Do This? 12
    Your Life 13

ORIENTATION 15

Getting Oriented 17

    Your Orientation 18
    Practice: External Orientation 19
    Practice: Internal Orientation 20
    Two Ingredients 21
    Who Are We? 22
    Cells 23
    Now 24
    Knowing About and Knowing 25
    On Truth 26
    Acting As If 27
    Practice: World's Safest Trust Fall 28
    Your Best Shot 29

Dangerous Questions 30
Listening 31

The Body 33

The Body and Creation 34
Practice: Feeling and Thinking 35
On Feeling 36
The Body as an Experience 37
Practice: Feet on the Floor 38
Holding Ambiguity 39
Practice: Two Hands 40
Practice: Feeling Your Project 41
Writing from the Body 42
How to Listen to a Body 43
Three Creative Centers 44
Embodied Cognition 46
The Body, Truth, and Direct Experience 47
Practice: The Body and Truth 48

Direct Experience 51

Direct Experience and Philosophy 52
A Quick Direct Experience Primer 53
What I Mean By Direct Experience 54
Posturing 55
The Grand Canyon 56
The Innocence of Direct Experience 57
Practice: Allowing Hearing and Seeing 58
Poetry 59
Your Direct Experience Is Not Confined to You 60
Noticing 61
The Anatomy of Noticing 62

Your Natural Voice 65

Your Natural Voice 66
Michelangelo's David 67

Phony 68
Your Natural Voice Is Not Something You Own 69
Safety 70
Authenticity 71
Revelation 72
Symptoms 73

ON CREATION 75

Before You Begin 76
How to Begin 77
When to Begin 78
Helpful, Kind, and True 79
Practice: Writing Truth 80
Dumb Questions 81
Action 82
Staying Motivated 83
Bold Assertions 84
Not Writing as Writing Practice 85
Sitting Quietly 86
Desire 87
On Desire: A Poem 88
Practice: Embodied Desire Through Breath 89
The Anatomy of Desire 90
Practice: Tending the Lower Belly 91
Practice: Desire as Fuel 92
Information Toxicity 93
Selective Hearing 94
Three Kinds of Medicine 95
Cliché 97
Personal Clichés 98
Practice: Liberating Cliché 100
Effort 101
Trying Hard 102
Putting on a Good Show 103
Practice: Dialogue 104
Paying Attention is Play .105
Simple and Complex 106

Restrictions 107
  Let It Breathe 108
  No Guarantees 109

DISORIENTATION 111

  Shocked Into Disorientation 113
  Free Fall 114
  Via Negativa 115
  Knowing Our Projects 116
  Terrible Feelings 117
  Turning Towards 119
  Turning Towards: A Thought Experiment 120
  Slowing Down and Decoupling 121
  The Periphery 123
  Antifragile 124
  Burn Everything You've Ever Done 125
  What Remains? 126

TOWARDS COMPLETION 129

  Some Questions You Could Ask Yourself at This Point .. 130
  Completion 131
  Completion and Saying No 132
  Last-Minute Additions 133
  The Last Two Percent 134
  On Sharing 135
  Vulnerable 136
  Affected 137
  Practice: Releasing and Receiving 138
  Compost 139
  Impact 140
  Letting Go 141
  And Now What? 142

Afterword
Gratitude

FOREWORD

by Brooke Thomas
Host of the *Liberated Being* podcast
and creator of the Embodied Practice studio

I'll often describe myself as a "maker." It's the best umbrella term I have for the number of individual and collaborative projects I have going at any given time — whether that's podcasting, teaching, developing a workshop, running an embodied practice studio, or supporting other "makers" in their work. Making stuff is one of the great drives and great joys of my life.

During one of these "making" adventures I had the great good fortune to co-create and co-teach a workshop, titled Living Your Body's Intelligence, with Liam. Collaborating can be a funny dance: you never really know how creation and communication styles sync up until you're actually in it. It begins as a leap of faith, always.

It was a leap I knew I could easily take with Liam. His thoughtfulness and integrity were palpable in every interaction I had had with him prior to our collaboration. And as the work began of putting together what we would teach — the where, how, and to whom — I was pleased to find a kindred maker-spirit in Liam.

Because of our current cultural norm of turning everything into inert objects to deliver to end users (thanks late capitalism!), people are often conditioned into creating things as if they were plastic objects to toss over an imagined fence to a crowd. Every new way of delivering the same plastic object becomes the new blueprint to follow.

In collaborating with Liam, I was thrilled to discover that he was able to do what many people have been habituated out of:

he could include the creative process as an alive and primary third party in our process of writing and co-teaching a class.

Liam has a gift for knowing how to connect with and listen to what wants to be born, rather than going through mechanical motions or performing a persona of who he is expected to be, or what the "end product" is supposed to be.

To be able to do this is actually a kind of alchemy. It keeps us from replicating yet more of the same, and instead allows for new things to come through whatever that creative portal is that brings freshness into the world.

This book feels like Liam was able to capture that felt process, usually impossibly wordless, and put it into words! On a page! A magical feat, truly.

For any fellow makers out there — whether you are a teacher, an entrepreneur, an artist, or engaged in any other kind of creative process (though personally I feel like this book could also just be a plain ol' guide to life), this book is a wonderful way to experientially drop you right into the flowing river of how to bring something forward.

This world needs us to stop recycling old ways and ideas. It needs the new to be born, and it is being born through us, the makers! So listen, attune, dive in, and see what's yours to bring through the creative portal with this wonderful book inviting you along every step of the way.

PREFACE

This book emerged during a radical turning in my life. I was soon to be turning 40, a new father, and recalibrating from a depression I'd experienced the year before. My life felt tumultuous and volatile, though I'd been surrendered in a way that felt deeply peaceful.

I took a morning walk with my son, as we often did and still do as of this writing. It's one of my favorite things in the world. He slept on my chest while I bounced rhythmically under an outdoor roof, watching and listening to the rain. I could tell my days as a bodyworker — my profession and passion for the previous ten years — were drawing to a close. I could feel that ending, but had no idea what was next.

I wondered, looking back, what have I done a lot of in this life? Images of creation began to emerge. I've crafted, and then delivered, a whole lot of classes. I began teaching martial arts when I was 15, and was creating curriculum for the 4-to-6 year old program by the end of that year. I spent thousands of hours teaching wilderness skills in the mountains and the desert in my twenties. My thirties were the decade of the soma: I was obsessed with the body, from anatomy to how a nervous system works to dancing, and guiding others to dance, with the myriad of bodily sensations as an inroad to healing.

All that time, I created and taught classes on the subjects I was immersed in. I put together hundreds of them, over tens of thousands of planning and teaching hours. The practice of creating these classes felt like a kind of training gym I would step into, time and time again. Sometimes I'd come out feeling bruised and defeated, other times feeling glowing and victorious. No matter the outcome, stepping into this training gym, the practice itself, was consistent.

There's a poem by Rilke in which he says,

> *I've been circling for thousands of years
> and I still don't know: am I a falcon, a storm,
> or a great song?*

As I held my son that day, I felt like I'd been circling something beautiful and essential. The practice of creation was something I had experienced many times, yet hadn't looked at directly.

This book is that looking. It's not really my tips and tricks from creating so many courses, because I don't have much of that kind of strategy. What's in these pages is what was left after the fires and the floods, the feel of skin sticky from evaporated sweat. It's mostly air, and scents you'll have to follow with your own nose.

Creating is a beautiful subject, I think, because it's such an internal process — it's *you* making something — and it's also so clearly in the world: it's you *making something*. It's not about what you think or believe; it's about what you do and how you do it. It's not philosophy; it's action.

I wrote this book for me as much as for anyone. I wanted a book I could open and have the sense of a good friend there with me, of wise council that wasn't trying to pep talk me or sell me anything. I wanted a book that wasn't afraid of the scary things that can emerge in the dark corners of my psyche, that knew more than I know.

May its pages, dear reader, be of benefit to you, too.

With love,
Liam

HOW TO USE THIS BOOK

You're holding a companion to accompany you along your creative projects. It could be happy living on your bookshelf, in your backpack, or right on the desk where you engage with your creative work. The flow of pages has a linearity — there's a beginning, middle, and end to roughly follow the beginning, middle, and end of making something — although you can open to any page and get a little reflection, like a tarot card.

Blessings on your way.

OPENING

THE CALL

Listen! The world calls you, in her myriad of voices, demands, pains, joys, the longings of our unlived lives. This is just the time to answer back, perhaps with a gesture, or a word, or with silence. You won't know ahead of time. From this point on you find out, moment by moment, who you are and what you are called to do.

You didn't miss anything. It's just beginning right now.

OPENING

A WALK IN THE WOODS

Let's call your creative project a walk in the woods. This book might be something of a tour guide.

This opening section is like the sign at the trailhead. Are you in the right place? Do you want to go on this hike? Here's the overview, the map of where we're going.

Orientation brings to light the context in which every step of the journey happens. It's the direction you're facing and how you might know that. It's the feel of your feet on the ground. It's how the dirt and trees smell so differently in early spring than late summer; what is the air like now? It's the smile, or scowl, or whatever it is on your face. It's where you just came from — signing your divorce papers? a week in Disneyland? — that informs your orientation right now.

The section on creation is most oriented towards the walking itself. This book is not "left foot, then right foot; watch for rocks!" It's for those who have walked a bit before.

Then we're out walking, having a fine time and . . . uh oh. *Rain clouds. I have a headache. Why did we do this stupid hike? We're lost, should've stayed home.* Disorientation may happen: doubts, dread, losing motivation, your entire psychic worldview crumbling in an instant, etc. It can feel terrible, though can be magical either because of some great epiphany you have in the thick of the hardship or, more commonly, you just muddle through it and somehow, drip by drip, the experience transforms you.

Thus, the section on disorientation is not about how to get reoriented per se. It's about being disoriented. To honor disorientation is not about pretending to like the rain if you don't. It's a gut-level acknowledgement that life can be deeply uncomfortable, and that alone doesn't mean anything has gone wrong.

Somehow, through grit and grace alike, we endure and find our way. We begin to attune towards the completion of this particular project-walk. And then, step by step, half an hour or six months later, there we are, stepping back out onto the trailhead.

That particular trip is gone forever. We may do many things from here, but we will never go on that exact walk again. You might have photos to show, or be able to write an article about it, but you know that's not the important part. The walking itself — in the wildness of nature — is complete unto itself. We walk in the woods to walk in the woods.

WHO THIS BOOK IS FOR

This book is for creators.

It's not about how to create anything you want.

It's about how to nurture that which wants to be born through you.

It's meant to be a companion in the wilderness where nothing is predictable, but we take the next step anyway.

It's for those who value a fruitful creative process over a nice-looking finished product, because you don't know how what you're making will be received, by yourself or anyone you share it with.

You might even die before your project is finished.

ON WRITING

"Writing" in this book refers to both the act of pen to paper, and to the general phenomenon of creation. In writing is the metaphor of first the blank page, then something on it. First there was no art installation; now there is. First there was no dinner on the table; now there is.

I've attempted in this book to stay true to my roots, my actual experiences centering around writing in the literal sense, while also staying true to my experience of writing as a general synonym with creation.

I hope this book serves you well, whatever the medium of your work.

ON METHOD

This book does not describe a replicable method of how to create something, because I do not have such a method. What has remained real and true through the fires of my life is not anything I can predict. Questions such as *do I create in the morning or the evening? how many hours per day? work on one project at a time or several at once?* certainly can be relevant to one's process, but I don't have a timeless answer for any of those.

Please don't mistake this openness for complacency. I can and do answer those questions on any given day, just as we all must if we are to be in the world of form and, therefore, preferences. I'm just telling you what I know, and I don't know a reliable method for a fruitful creative process.

This book is a look at what underscores method.

CREATION'S PROCESS

This creation process, at its most fundamental, is happening in ways infinite and too intricate to fathom. Consider how we breathe, how we walk, how we wash the dishes, how we raise our children and our neighbor's children, are all acts of creation.

Where it comes from and what it means is not my domain. This book is about the process itself.

OPENING

CREATING AS A PRACTICE

Cultivating a regular practice can be a wonderful thing. Creation can be such a practice.

Any dedicated practitioner will undergo ups and downs throughout the days, weeks, years of practice. But neither up nor down is the point; they're just movements the boat makes on the ocean. Getting to know the ocean is the point.

SURFING

I think surfing is a really good metaphor for creating something.

Do you have to do something to surf? Yes, of course.

Yet, just as obvious is the fundamental element of the ocean, the medium you are engaged in and its currents that are far too complex and generational to ever fully understand. The sea itself is completely out of your control.

There are times when it's appropriate to bust your ass to get out beyond the break. There are times when it's best to sit and wait, and you might as well enjoy the air and the feel of the water, the song of seagulls while you're there. There are times to paddle at just the right cadence to catch a wave.

It's the same basic idea every time, but it's never the same experience, is it?

This book is not about surfing, but it is about finding right effort in a vast ocean.

ROSES

This practice is one of letting your innate intelligence fruit into the world.

Just as we could say a rose likes to do its rose thing — that is to say it looks, feels, and smells like a rose — so do you and I long to express in our particular way.

A rose doesn't seem to have in mind where it's going, though its form expresses an unimaginably coherent intelligence. Here, it's appearing as a rose. It as me looks like me; as you it looks like you.

We already are this intelligence. The practice is its fruition.

OPENING

WHY DO THIS?

Affirmation is a fickle fuel source. This is a book for those more interested in trust, desire, and love.

Trust that something wants to be born through you. Trust that you not only don't need to see, but can't see, the entirety of what's happening, of all that you're a part of. Thank goodness. You can just relax and do your part, but a note in a chord in a cosmic choir — with the added bonus of getting to hear the whole song, composed and played in real time!

When it all ends in dust, why create at all? Because you desire it. Because we are creative beings, and you feel compelled to. There are no accolades, nor anyone to blame. We do these projects because we want to.

And that's love: to share what's real as a primal impulse.

> *Even after all this time,*
> *the Sun never says to the Earth,*
> *"You owe me."*
>
> — Hafiz

OPENING

YOUR LIFE

Whatever happens in your life while you're working is part of the work itself. This has nothing to do with being vulnerable, or transparent. It's just naming that where you live, who's around you, the mood you're in, what your great-grandparents went through, the way the wind is blowing, and what you had for breakfast are all a part of this creation, too.

There are far too many variables to keep track. Consider the extent to which we can find a wholehearted agreement with what is right now — to say yes to your life, just as I must say yes to mine — is the extent to which we are resourced to engage with the world.

The world is perfect as it is, including my desire to change it.

— Ram Dass

ORIENTATION

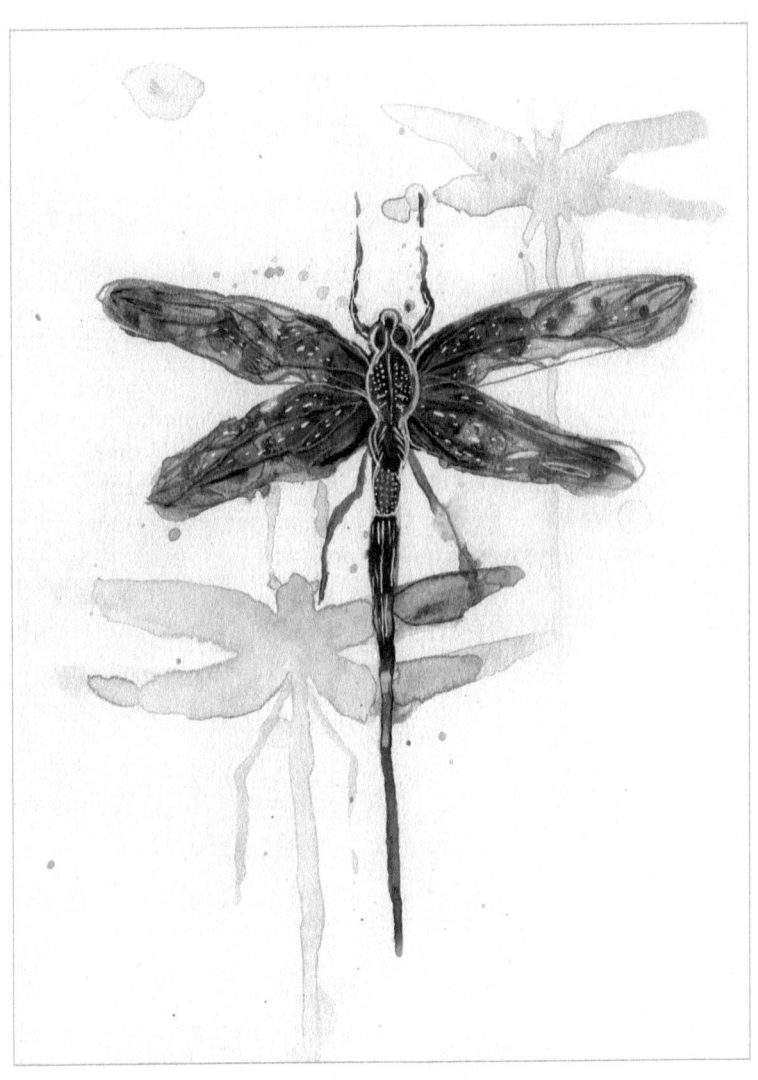

Orientation is what is before you begin.

It's not a destination, not even a movement. It's the direction you're facing, the particular predispositions from which movement unfolds.

This section is in four parts: Getting Oriented, The Body, Direct Experience, and Your Natural Voice. You could think of these parts as different vantages from which we gaze into one thing: your relationship to everything within and without you.

ORIENTATION
Getting Oriented

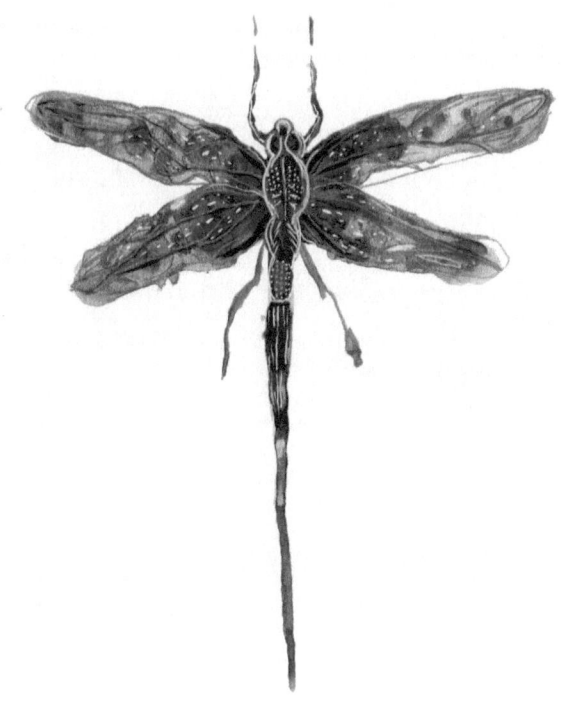

YOUR ORIENTATION

Your particular orientation is yours to experience, one moment at a time.

When we're not pretending to be somewhere else, here reveals itself most fully.

Here, there's generally less conflict between the way we're seeing things and the way things are. The practice of creation can then feel a bit more vital than draining, more an expression of an innate life-force than a bunch of random events, more like our hearts speaking in different tongues than the discord of an ominous soundtrack.

PRACTICE: EXTERNAL ORIENTATION

[A lack of appreciation for the] underlying unity between organism and environment is a dangerous hallucination.

— Alan Watts

Orientation can refer equally to how you are, on the inside, and where you are, on the outside. This practice is about orienting to the outside.

Using your whole body to turn, look around the space you're in. If you're in a room, look at all its corners. Look especially behind you, and in any dark places.

This external orientation practice is two things:

> 1. It's an embodied acknowledgement that we don't create in vacuums; we create in particular spaces, each with their own physicality, mood, energy, and history.

> 2. It's a way of helping your deep animal self feel more safe. (We all have a large amount of our subconscious perception devoted to surveying for danger. Search the internet for "neuroception" for more on this topic.)

Consider doing this anytime you're feeling skittish, and each time before you begin your creation practice.

PRACTICE: INTERNAL ORIENTATION

Once you've oriented to the space you're in, consider feeling into the particulars of your inner orientation, your internal posture, before even contemplating the subject of your project.

> *How* are you beginning?
>
> What's the texture-feeling of what it's like to be you right now?
>
> Do you feel relaxed, open? . . . guarded, angry? . . . foggy, confused?

The words here are just pointers. The objective isn't to pick a category; it's to sense the water you're swimming in — to feel the water's temperature and its many layers of current. The point is to be affected before attempting to affect.

You are not searching for anything hidden, only what's obvious.

It's common to dismiss this obviousness, and want to get on with something more expressive. Consider with your bones and heart right now that whatever wants to be born through you is right here, so you needn't hurry in its direction.

Take another moment to relax, not to dull your senses or try to not think, but to thrive as the bubbling wellspring of creation itself. However you are is how it is expressing through you at this moment. What's it like to create as this, that you are and need not seek?

TWO INGREDIENTS

This practice of creation calls for two ingredients in equal proportion.

1. Deeply, passionately care about the quality of your work and how it's received. Do your absolute best, every time.

2. Don't give a hoot what your work looks like or how it's received. Don't try very hard, if at all, to create it. Let it come as easily as a falling leaf in autumn.

One of these without the other is lacking. Both are essential.

WHO ARE WE?

It's exhausting to know yourself only as a self-serving entity, bestowing gifts or carnage on other self-serving entities. I've found that creating something solely from this vantage will feel incomplete, no matter what I've made.

A self-serving nature makes sense in a certain context — food, clothing, and shelter are wonderfully personal — but its reach is limited, is it not? It tends not to go deep into the soil of our hearts, where our roots are hopelessly intertwined with the roots of all other beings.

This is not a nice idea; it's the truth as far as I can tell.

To live that truth is liberation from ourselves. We have the strength of the whole universe for whatever task is called for. The doing is not defined by effort.

To deny that truth and live only as a dog eating other dogs is when effort really feels like effort, like you are some lonely sludge, slugging it out against gravity. It's lonely even when you win.

We can inquire into the truth of this, and create from that understanding.

> *Why are you unhappy? Because 99% of what you do is for yourself, and there isn't one.*
>
> — Wei Wu Wei

ORIENTATION

CELLS

Imagine you are a liver cell.

You chat with a kind of cell that makes foot bones.

You both describe your work, your lives, how you see things, what's important to you. You likely find there are tremendous differences between you on all of these topics.

What a difference it would be if one or both of you knew you were orchestrated by the same mysterious intelligence that animates a human body.

Without it, you'd seem miles apart. With that one insight, you'd know: *oh, you are doing just what you should be doing! Down there, making bone, so different than me up here doing the cleansing stuff of a liver.*

We have trillions of "competing priorities" in our bodies every second. And yet, somehow, there's an unimaginably smooth organization of it all.

Neither you nor I has to define what kind of cell we are. We just need to, or at least get the opportunity to, do what comes naturally to us. It's the same gesture as letting others do the same.

NOW

This conversation we are having, you and I and the universe over, is only happening right now.

Now is not a quick blip, some thin slice of time sandwiched between the yawning abysses of past and future. It's a hum, a constant ongoing. Now is the only time you and I have ever experienced anything.

What's it like now? What's the texture of the page, the weight of this book in your hands like? Any bit of now can be a doorway into all of it.

This is about creating a better future, and neither you nor I know what that future will be. The only thing we can be certain of is it will arise out of now.

> *Forever – is composed of Nows –*
> *'Tis not a different time –*
>
> — Emily Dickinson

ORIENTATION

KNOWING ABOUT AND KNOWING

There are two ways to know a river.

One is to read about it. Think about it. Measure it from afar.

The other is to sit by it, listen to it, watch it, be consumed and confused by it, annoyed by it, inquire into what it is besides something you perceive. This is more like you would listen to a friend than you would study an object.

Both of these ways of knowing something are legitimate. The second one, the sitting by, is pretty different though, eh? It's more a *getting to know* than a *knowing about.*

And after years of sitting by the same river, you might not have much to say when asked what you know about it. But you might. (Let's go find out.)

ON TRUTH

This book is full of me saying *this is the way things are.*

What I say may not be true in your experience.

Consider two reactions upon hearing any assertion.

Perhaps you agree. You feel what I'm saying is true because it lights something up for you, or it's just already obvious to you.

Or perhaps you say *no, that's not the way it is. My actual experience is . . .*

Either one of those outcomes is a good one in my book. These words are alive inasmuch as they evoke a living response, and that aliveness is what matters.

ACTING AS IF

To trust something wants to be born through you even when it doesn't feel like it is a massive act of aspiration.

It's not a sedative.

True faith doesn't say *well, it's all taken care of so I'm just going to kick back and not do anything.*

How boring is that, anyway?

True faith says *I don't know the way, I can't even see the way, but I'm going to take this next step.*

What's the next step? Whatever you're experiencing right now, which includes what you're doing, and if and how you feel compelled to move.

Let the rest be taken care of. Act as if it is and see what happens.

PRACTICE: WORLD'S SAFEST TRUST FALL

Lie on the ground in any position that's comfortable. You could also sit.

Feel your body falling towards, and simultaneously being caught by, the ground.

Notice if, and where and how, you are pulling away from the ground, recoiling like someone not quite ready to jump off a diving board. Allow that tension as best as you can. Keep focusing on the feeling of support from the ground, and tending kindly to your bodily response.

It's the world's safest trust fall.

When you get up, notice in what ways the support of the floor is still there. You are still in a bit of a trust fall, every step.

. . .

What we're after here is neither release, nor trust; we're after clear perception. Trust might result from clear perception, but trust can't be forced. It does not unfold on our timeline. You are trillions of self-aware cells. It's natural there will be variance in their preferences.

> *Thanks to Brooke Thomas for giving me the delightful name for this exercise*

ORIENTATION

YOUR BEST SHOT

Is your project going to turn out great or terribly?

Can you see how optimism and pessimism in this instance serve the same function? They're both ways of (attempting to) avoid the relationships, and therefore the uncertainties, inherent in our work.

The only real answer is you don't know how it will turn out. No one knows.

What remains now besides giving it your best shot?

ORIENTATION

DANGEROUS QUESTIONS

We could consider the questions posed in this book as rhetorical in the original spirit of rhetoric: more about the conversation they produce than a tidy monologue-as-answer.

At best, an open, rhetorical question like "what is that like for you?" is an intriguing invitation, and yields insight that might not have arisen otherwise. At worst, an open question like that lacks vitality and fosters what is, for most of us, an all-too-familiar tailspin, listening to ourselves say the same things we've said a million times before.

It's not that some questions are good and some aren't. It's how a question lands with us, and to what degree we're affected by searching for its answer.

To that end, we could consider the questions posed in this book as potentially dangerous questions, the kind of question than can upend you. I was so taken by this bundling of words in the following excerpt, in which spiritual teacher Adyashanti is asked a question by one of his students.

The student asks about the nature of enlightenment: "What is liberated from what?"

Adya answers the student, "that sort of question is what you're liberated from. Be sincere; don't ask questions out of mere interest. Ask dangerous questions — the ones whose answers could change your life."

This is not about bravado. We could also simply say: consider asking the questions you actually care about, not just the ones that tidy up the room.

ORIENTATION

LISTENING

Is listening the same thing as being able to recall what the speaker just said? Is there a quality to it that's more than that?

A few considerations as you listen to the myriad of voices around you: Listening is a willingness, if not a longing, to be affected by what you hear. It is a vibrant silence, not just a dead space defined by lack of speaking. You are listening to the extent you're willing to hear absolutely anything.

> *How do I listen?*
> *As if everyone were my Master*
> *speaking to me his cherished last words.*
>
> — Hafiz

ORIENTATION
The Body

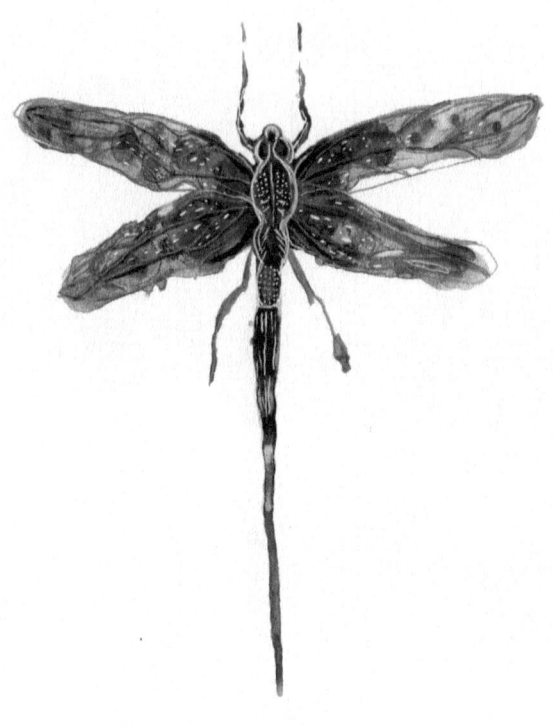

THE BODY AND CREATION

We all know what it's like to create from disembodied concepts, to attempt to copy something we already know. Memory serves very well to reproduce what has happened before, but creation by its nature is not what has happened before.

The body is always new territory, an antenna tuned to here and now.

ORIENTATION

PRACTICE: FEELING AND THINKING

Feel your right hand over the course of a few breaths. You are feeling anything that is a direct experience in the area of your right hand: warmth, coolness, pain, tingling, dullness, a vacuousness.

Now think about your right hand.

What's the difference?

ON FEELING

Four notes on feeling.

1. *To feel* is an interesting verb in the English language. The same word can mean the experience of feeling an object, like you feel the skin of an orange, or it can refer to something you feel from the inside, like a headache. I'll be using the word to refer to the inner experience.

2. Feeling is the language with which your body speaks: tingling, heat, coolness, aches, pleasures, and pains. Even feelings that don't make sense can still be sensory experiences: thickness or thinness, space, viscosity, colors.

3. Bodily sensations and the accompanying emotions are synonymous through a physio-anatomical lens. The pounding heart *is* the anxiety; they are one and the same. Though there is no floating entity called "anxiety" in the body, there is an area called "the heart." And we can feel that area. You can experience your body in real time, as opposed to a concept which lies outside of any particular place or time context.

4. Working with your feelings can be quite powerful. Powerful doesn't mean better. If any exercise is overwhelming and you want to stop, stop.

ORIENTATION

THE BODY AS AN EXPERIENCE

Your bodily experience is yours alone to know. It's really useful to trust it. Your ability to perceive clearly, and to create from that clearer perception, may grow as your trust deepens.

It's common for many of us to default to the thought that we're not doing it good enough, that we should be feeling more subtly, feeling different things in different areas, experiencing more flow, etc. None of that matters.

If you have a hard time feeling your body, try completing this sentence: "I can't feel anything; all I notice is . . ." The *all I notice is* is it. It can seem too simple, too obvious, too available to be what you're looking for. But that's it. What is that really like — the dullness, the lack of sensation, the ordinariness of it?

Your body is as you experience it, right now. You are both the observer and that which is being observed.

Consider this kind of attentive experience as a basic orientation.

ORIENTATION

PRACTICE: FEET ON THE FLOOR

Feel your feet on the floor.

Notice if this is your perspective: you are up here, receiving information from your feet, which are down there.

See if you can sense directly a self-awareness in the cells of your feet. From this perspective, you are are not feeling the feet from a distance; you are the feet, feeling themselves.

This is not about bringing consciousness down into your feet. What you are looking for, the aliveness and awareness, is already there.

HOLDING AMBIGUITY

The logic of thought seeks clarity and resolution. If there are two opposing viewpoints, only one of them can be correct.

The logic of the body is more ambiguous. You can desire, for example, several competing priorities at once.

Consider how ambiguity in your work may not be a weakness. Ambiguity makes something harder to summarize, but how do you summarize a living body with any grace?

PRACTICE: TWO HANDS

Bring your attention to your right hand. Remember the distinction between *thinking about* and *feeling directly* your right hand. Feel what's there.

Now bring your attention to your left hand. Spend a few breaths feeling here.

Now feel both hands at once.

Notice this obvious truth: you can feel your right hand as your right hand, and your left hand as your left hand. You are experiencing two phenomena at once, yet there is only one experience happening.

To embody this, bring both your hands together, in front of your heart in a prayer position.

Notice you still have a right hand, and a left hand, and you now have the experience of two hands together. None of these contradict each other.

PRACTICE: FEELING YOUR PROJECT

Think about your project. Hold it in your mind's eye. Notice what's there — perhaps images, words, timelines, lists of what to do.

Notice what, if any, sensation is evoked by this thinking. Excitement? Worry? Detachedness? Not much?

Let's call this what it is: the sensations arising when you think about your project.

Now notice if there is any sense of being able to feel into your project itself, the same way you felt into your own hands and feet. Is there a kind of consciousness there that you can directly experience?

Is it so important for this practice to suspend belief, whether that belief is that you can or can't do this. Belief isn't important here; direct experience is.

WRITING FROM THE BODY

Let sensation guide you. Where are you drawn, towards and away from? Remember acting here is never about a final answer, or even a destination, but is an impetus for movement that has its own wisdom.

Let your palate guide you. What tastes sweet? What tastes bitter like green plants in springtime? What tastes like a bunch of baloney, the kind of white-bread sandwich your mom used to make but isn't really what your palate craves right now?

Let your embodied imagination guide you. What can you sense-imagine as a gift, for yourself or for others, as if it were already so? What aspirations tickle the outskirts of your thoughtforms, as if to say *we're on our way...*

HOW TO LISTEN TO A BODY

Your body speaks in a myriad of sensation-feeling languages. It may be barely perceptible, a feeling of the faintest inner breeze. It may also be overt, a banging of a deep drum in your chest.

Listening is already happening.

Listen like you'd listen to the sounds of nature if you just sat down in the deep forest. You may hear sounds of animals, or not, but it's not like you're sitting there impatiently, waiting for a certain bird to chirp. You're just relaxing, and listening, feeling whatever is around and within you.

Don't demand that certain sensations arise and that others go away, or that your breath go to a particular place. Your bodily experience is immensely mysterious and vast. Experience the ordinary here and see what happens.

Don't ask about what you're not experiencing that you could be. Ask what you are experiencing.

THREE CREATIVE CENTERS

We could consider the cranium and its contents as the centerpiece of the intellect. The largest organ here is the brain. It's the elements of air and space. Bring your attention to the voluminous contents of your skull. What's it like to see and feel the world from here?

Let your attention now rest in the center of your ribcage. The heart-lungs most embody our emotions. We're in the elements of fire and water, like a volcano. Is this an accessible area? Sense what is already there, like we did with our feet in the earlier chapter. You don't need to go into your heart. You already are your heart. What's it like to see and feel the world from this place?

Now bring your attention to the lower belly. Perhaps give a little rub to the skin there just below your belly button. What is underneath that skin? And deep to that . . . all the way back to your sacrum. Experience yourself as the center volume of this area. This is existential territory, the seat of life, deep waters, and earth. How does the world look from here?

The head, heart, and pelvis are the three centers in many traditions of healing. For our practice of creation, consider the exercises above as quick primers that might inform creating from your whole self.

Lastly, please remember these divisions are just concepts, images meant to evoke a certain perspective. Anatomically, your brain, heart, and connective tissues of your pelvis are present in every square inch, every nook and cranny, of your body.

We grew from a seed, as all living things do, and these systems are not separate. Your heart is full of neurons; your brain is full of blood. This exercise is not because there's somewhere you need to go in your body. It's just shining the light on the centerpiece expressions.

EMBODIED COGNITION

Your body's physiological processes affect, perhaps even solely define, what you think and feel. You will think different thoughts when you're holding a warm cup of tea on a cold day than if you're not. Another example is how most of us find it easier to get angry when we're hungry.

Your overt movement or positions also affect what you think and feel. You will think different thoughts when you're sitting than when you're walking. Raising your arms above your head, proudly in a victorious gesture, might make you feel different than when your hands are resting at your side. (This is a free, two-second experiment. Try it!)

The field of embodied cognition can lead to endless neurotic tinkering with one's posture and movement. It can also point more simply to the bodymind, not two things that we need to join, but one thing that was never not one thing, that here looks like "body" and here looks like "mind."

Consider either expression an equally valid access point into the one thing, into the other.

If you're feeling stuck on your project, take a walk.

THE BODY, TRUTH, AND DIRECT EXPERIENCE

The body is how you experience, and what you directly experience is what is true.

I'm not saying that what we think about what we just experienced is true.

I'm also not saying that if something is outside of your direct experience it, therefore, isn't true. But whatever that is is for other people to talk about, and for you and me to listen to.

PRACTICE: THE BODY AND TRUTH

Bring your attention to your body. Note that you're not *thinking about* your body; you are *feeling as* your body.

Say something true. "My name is . . ."

Pause and feel for a few breaths.

Now say something you know to be untrue. It might make it more real if you imagine someone asked you a question, and you're now answering them untruthfully, with the intent to deceive. (This can feel remarkably unsettling!)

Pause and feel as your body for a few breaths.

Were those different experiences?

You can repeat this exercise and try it with more subtle (and more personal) forms of truth telling. As you're creating, consider this a guide: if and when you feel a bodily sense of tension, drain, or fatigue, it may be worth pausing your work and inquiring into if you're saying anything untrue.

* Thanks to Paul Linden for introducing me to this investigation

*It takes a certain maturity of mind to accept
that nature works as steadily in rust as in rose petals.*

— Esther Warner Dendel

ORIENTATION
Direct Experience

DIRECT EXPERIENCE AND PHILOSOPHY

This book is for those seeking to create more from direct experience than from philosophy. It's the difference between walking into the wilderness seeing what's in front of you — your direct experience — versus walking into the wilderness with your eyes fixed behind you, looking at the terrain you encountered moments, seconds, or years before, thinking you know what's coming up because of where you've been.

What you encounter next may be nothing like what you've ever seen.

Philosophy says, "this is what I believe about how the world works." It is informed by what has happened. There's nothing wrong with philosophy; your beliefs shape the content of your creation.

Direct experience says nothing. While you can speak *from* your direct experience, the phenomenon itself is pure perception.

A QUICK DIRECT EXPERIENCE PRIMER

Find any bit of food you have nearby.

Think about what it would be like to eat it. Imagine what it might taste like. You are experiencing your imagination.

Now take a bite, taste, and chew.

That's direct experience.

WHAT I MEAN BY DIRECT EXPERIENCE

Direct experience, as I'll be talking about it, refers more to a feeling sense than a binary statement of *yes, I have actually done that* or *no, I haven't*.

It's not like you are forbidden from writing about mountains if you haven't spent time in the mountains. Your longing for the mountains is a direct experience. Your imagination about the mountains is a direct experience. Your fears and hopes, even your speculations, about something are as real as anything.

But when we are in an age where it is easier than ever to fool ourselves about what we really feel, it's nice to have some verbiage to point in the direction of authenticity.

There's a saying in Zen that "you can't eat the menu." It means reading about concepts is not the same as experiencing them, just as reading about an orange is not the same as eating an orange. Though it's funny because you could, of course, eat the menu. You would be eating a menu. So long as you weren't trying to convince yourself or anyone else that you were actually eating the reality pointed to by the words printed on the paper, there's no problem.

POSTURING

I don't know about you, but I find it unnervingly easy to speak outside of my direct experience.

I don't mean I just make stuff up, pretending it were true. It's more like an impulse to avoid the difficult parts of life, to jump ahead to where I'm The Guy Who Knows Things. I want to be The Guy Who Has Achieved the Great Achievement and can now sit in a special chair and dispel wisdom. It feels like a scared corner of my psyche that says *I want to have done it, but not really to do it.*

Bless the tenderness of this place. I've come to find out, though, that as much as I want to stay safe, even more than that I want to participate in life's unfolding. Perhaps you want that, too.

THE GRAND CANYON

Imagine how much you could talk about the Grand Canyon if you'd read a 300-page book about it. Someone asks you after you finished the book, "What's the Grand Canyon like?"

You could likely talk at length if you so chose. "It's this deep and this wide and the rock is like this, the water flows like this..."

Now, imagine you haven't read anything about it, but you spend a month immersed, backpacking through it. Someone asks you now, "What's the Grand Canyon like?"

It's not that it's dishonest to speak about the Grand Canyon in the example where you'd only read the book, but that knowledge should not be confused with the knowing from the other experience. Breadth and depth are two different dimensions.

If you should find yourself posturing like you know something deeply that you don't, let's celebrate together. Perhaps the seeing allows some relaxation of your grip on trying to prove something, as it has for me. Relaxing in this way might allow us a more honest, and thorough, look at what's really around and within us.

ORIENTATION

THE INNOCENCE OF DIRECT EXPERIENCE

Everything you, me, and our mothers experienced, we have done so innocently. It's worth steeping in this recognition for a moment or two.

What you see, what you hear, as well as what you feel and think: how could any of this be otherwise? It's as innocent as seeing a chair in a room: you see it, that form over there. This is to say nothing of the fact that you can now move the chair to another room if you wish. Or you can ignore it, or pretend it's your grandfather.

The nature of how you saw that form, that for shorthand we call "chair," is purely innocent. It just sees.

Your hearing just hears. Wonderful and terrible thoughts arrive and the first, fundamental truth of the situation is you see them. That perception itself is completely innocent, is it not? (We can, perhaps, do all kinds of non-innocent things from there.)

Bathe in this innocence, like warm waters, from time to time.

PRACTICE: ALLOWING HEARING AND SEEING

Sit or stand comfortably. What do you see?

Bring your attention to the very simple fact that you don't need to strain to see what you see. You don't need to go out and get it, either literally or as a subtle energetic thing. You can just relax, eyes open, and the seeing happens quite on its own.

Now, let sound come. Notice if there are parts of your experience that strain to hear. Bring attention to the fact that you can hear if you do strain. You can also hear if you don't strain. Sound is coming to you, without any effort on your part.

This practice works just as well with any other sense.

POETRY

If you haven't already, consider seeking out a poem or two today as a teacher and friend.

Poetry is a different use of language than prose. A good poem is not easily summarized. Its particular words, their shape and cadence, are as much the poem as the poem's subject is.

A poem is not defined by its structure. It can be two words or a hundred pages; the length isn't the point. What the poem evokes is the point. The words are tools to sculpt something, and should be put away when the sculpture is complete.

Try writing one. Don't write it for an audience, not even for yourself for later. Write a poem in honor of now, for now. What do you see in the room you're in? What do you hear? What's arising in you? See what comes out. Then burn it.

YOUR DIRECT EXPERIENCE IS NOT CONFINED TO YOU

Your direct experience does not exclude the outside world.

Someone telling you something is part of it. To dismiss anything you don't like by saying "well, that's not my experience" is missing the point, and equally as nonsensical as agreeing with everyone all the time. It doesn't mean you necessarily agree with what they're saying. It means you're acknowledging its place in the universe.

When we talk about your direct experience in this book, it includes and is informed by your particular predispositions — likes, aversions, and all the rest — though it is not limited to them. Your direct experience comes before choice, and thus is not limited to what you agree with.

In fact, if you are creating from the whole of your direct experience, there's almost certainly going to be elements of the work that you don't understand, perhaps even feel contradictory to.

Don't keep those parts merely because they're contradictory. Keep them if they're true and necessary.

NOTICING

Our experiences seem dull when they are categorical. Say you and I are sitting on a grassy hill one evening. I'm looking down at my phone. You notice the sky's brilliance and say to me, "wow, check out that sunset." I may look up and notice that, in fact, it is a sunset happening, just like you said. Red, orange, sun low in the sky... got it. Then back to my phone.

If I'm lucky, the sunset may be enough to jar me for a moment into an experience I could never fully put into words. Never. Not even if I spent a lifetime writing about that one sunset alone, there would always be more to say about the subtle changing of colors, what the air felt like, our companionship in that moment, the way the grass was growing and insects were dying, and how our planet hummed through the cosmos.

All in one word: sunset.

To say "notice this," then, is an odd thing. It's not asking us to look for something hidden in the traditional sense. It's not like something was hidden about the sunset from me if I had just glanced. I did notice it. I just wasn't impressed. Perhaps I wasn't impressed because it was unimpressive, but maybe I wasn't impressed because I didn't allow it to impress upon me.

Whatever we call that letting in, the kind of noticing that arises from love, curiosity, or disorientation — where you don't know *what* to look for anymore — let's give our attention to that.

> *The Kingdom of Heaven is spread out over the whole earth, yet men do not see it.*
>
> — Jesus, in the Gospel of Thomas

ORIENTATION

THE ANATOMY OF NOTICING

Your nervous system is the mouth and ears of your inner self.

About half of your nerve tissue runs from nerve endings in your muscles, bones, connective tissues, and organs back into your brain and spine. These — the afferent or sensory nerves — carry outside information in. When you're noticing a sunset, that is a lot of what you're noticing with.

The other half of this nerve tissue runs from your brain and spinal cord out to the muscles, bones, connective tissues, and organs. These — called efferent or motor nerves — carry impulses from the central nervous system out.

All these nerves relate to each other in mind-bogglingly complex ways; some of those relationships deepen over time and become easier to access. It's how we learn. There's a saying in physical medicine that "neurons that fire together, wire together." It means the more you do something a certain way, or notice something a certain way, the more habituated your nervous system becomes to doing it, or perceiving it, that same way again.

This has an upside: we no longer have to think about how to lift a cup to drink from it. It also has a cost: we tend not to notice the world as freshly as we once did, back when we had to because it was all new.

But take heart; there are no literal wires in your nervous system, and these neural relationships are malleable to your last breath. There's always another chance to notice what's really here, and that chance is now.

Everything you add to the truth subtracts from the truth.

— Alexander Solzhenitsyn

ORIENTATION
Your Natural Voice

YOUR NATURAL VOICE

From a relishing in the innocence of your direct bodily experience may arise a kind of natural voice in your creation work.

It's natural because it feels natural to you. In the same way you look in the mirror and say "oh, that's me" without needing to think about it, your natural voice feels like "oh, that's my voice" without needing to think about it.

It is not the memory of another voice, someone else's or your own.

Your natural voice is like the wind. You'll never capture it, or even see it. You can only see and feel its presence by experiencing how it interacts with something else.

MICHELANGELO'S DAVID

I love the story of Michelangelo's famous sculpture, David.

Legend has it, when asked how he created such a perfect work of art, the artist replied that "David was already in the marble. My task was to remove all the stone that wasn't him."

In a world of additions — of more, better, faster — it is worth considering your natural voice as a demolition project. I have found this to be true, often with much protest on my part, that life will strip all but my essential voice from me. It's the only thing left when everything has fallen away, probably because it's not a thing. The natural voice is primordial, and how it may reveal itself to us, and through us, is unpredictable.

PHONY

The opposite of natural is phony.

Phony is a sense that only you will know for you, just as only I will know it for me.

Phony is when, however wonderful your words may sound, there's a nagging sense of disconnect, of needing to try to live up to someone else's standards. Phony is partnered with cliché, and with the kind of cleverness where you're working to impress more than illuminate.

There's no beating phony. There's just surrender to the removal process, slowly and surely revealing your natural voice.

YOUR NATURAL VOICE IS NOT SOMETHING YOU OWN

Your natural voice is not something you own. Yours doesn't belong to you just as mine doesn't belong to me.

It can be useful to be able to quickly pitch your ideas. *Here's who I am; here's what I'm about.* But that's just a summary based on what has happened. You don't know what your natural voice will say next. It's not something you command.

What if you awaken tomorrow to find a completely different sense of yourself?

A lovely, unnerving question posed by one of my teachers: what if you received the answer from God that fulfilling your highest purpose was to do some dull and dreary job for the rest of your life?

The lark, of course, is that no one knows. It's a verb continuously revealing itself. There's no "the rest of your life." There's just this.

SAFETY

If you've ever been really scared, you know no amount of pep talk will get you safely through it. Being afraid is a brainstem, root-chakra, animal experience in which rational thought is the observer, not the driver.

Speaking — whether out loud or in writing — in your natural voice can be really scary.

You may have been told as a child, "you're being too much right now, calm down" or any number of restraints that, however innocently administered, can be quite traumatizing for a young psyche.

That trauma, that same feeling response that arose when you were told you were too much, can be present in your bodymind now as much as it was then. You feel it now because it's coming up for air and for love, not to ruin your life.

Don't pep talk yourself any more than is helpful. Consider, if you're feeling stuck in a project, doing a thing or two that helps you feel safe.

Orient to the room, take a warm shower and feel the heat, get a solid hug from a good friend. A list of options is only useful to the extent you're able to directly, personally experience if it's helping or not. Let your own sense of safety be the guide.

You may find, as I have, that when your natural voice feels more safe to come out, you don't need to motivate it nearly as much as we might have believed.

ORIENTATION

AUTHENTICITY

Authenticity is an inner game, entirely. It's something for you to know for you, and me to know for me, and not to make a show about.

REVELATION

Revelatory experiences are not your natural voice.

An experience wherein everything makes sense in the world, however brief, can be tremendously blissful.

But when things go back to normal, yesterday's revelation can be today's curse to the extent we try to recreate it.

Trying to produce revelation asks, "what isn't here?"

Your authentic voice asks, "what is?"

SYMPTOMS

There are some classic signs and symptoms of your natural voice being freer to flower on its own terms.

You may experience joy and uplift, a sense of having a weight off your chest, a choke removed from your throat. You may feel the wondrous connection of being part of something greater, of what you do being orchestrated by a larger intelligence. You may experience less fear of saying what you really feel, and less agitation when others express how they really feel.

You may experience bodily pain, as deep glaciers begin to flow, ossified beds begin to shift. You may experience flutters of anxiety, even terror, as what was buried deep in your body since long ago rushes forth to bathe in this light of loving permission you've been tending to. You may feel disoriented, physically — less coordinated, memory less sharp, a kind of nauseating spin in your cranium — as old points of orientation liquify. Your close relationships may be called to new levels of honesty, and that can be really scary.

How long any of these symptoms last is not for us to know. There's no going back, though.

ON CREATION

BEFORE YOU BEGIN

Before you begin your work, each time, consider:

Orient to the space you'll be creating in, and with.

Ask, "who might this work serve?" Feel that innate impulse, longing to serve strangers as well as you serve those you love.

Begin with a ritual of any kind. These are best if they're something you do, not just think. A few ideas:

- take five slow breaths
- take a bow
- bring your hands together and smile
- light a candle
- ring a bell
- say out loud "I am beginning today's practice of creation"

- or simply do what it is you already do to begin your work day, just give it the loving attention you'd give any ritual

End your session with something, too. It can be the same thing you opened with.

HOW TO BEGIN

Too late. Your project has already begun, has it not? The daydreaming, the doubts, the unrequited cravings, seeds sown when you were a child, perhaps even generations before you . . . it's all well underway.

May we align our will and cognition with the currents of life already moving.

ON CREATION

WHEN TO BEGIN

Begin when you have something to say.

It doesn't need to be — it isn't — the final word. It's a moment in a conversation.

How do you know when you have something to say? Use the same intuition that would inform you in conversation with a good friend. This is someone you don't need to impress. Though you may impress them with what you say, it's not the orientation for when and how to speak.

What you say in this conversation will depend entirely on the context of what you and your friend are talking about. Where that context informs what's arising in you — what you actually think and feel — is where content comes from.

Begin when you actually have something to say.

HELPFUL, KIND, AND TRUE

It's an old adage with many variations, a kind of check and balance system to the infinite pitfalls of conditioning, of a hardened heart masquerading as knowledge. The verbiage that most resonates with me right now asks *is what I'm saying now helpful? is it kind? is it true to the best of my knowing?*

If yes to all of these, green light.

> **Helpful:** not flashy, not impressive, but helpful.
>
> **Kind:** having the best interest of others on the forefront of my heart and mind.
>
> **True:** representing what I know, to the best of my ability, to be true. This may or may not be what anyone else likes or agrees with. Speaking truth when it most matters often feels like a confession to me.

All of these words point to where the material is originating from inside the creator. It's not something to get right. Consider these three gates as a three-headed friend who loves you no matter what, beyond reason, who will keep asking you direct, honest questions and who you most honor by giving direct, honest answers — silently, in your own heart — in return.

ON CREATION

PRACTICE: WRITING TRUTH

Sit down with a pen and paper. Write only what you know to be true.

When you notice yourself, however subtly, beginning to veer into glossed-over mental landscapes — sometimes for me it's a sense that I'm beginning to perform or tidy things up — stop writing.

Only begin again when you have something true to say. And again, when you notice the veneer of disconnect from your actual experience, just stop. Don't go anywhere, physically or mentally, just stop right there. Breathe and metabolize your experience, whatever is arising.

It's a funny thing to talk about, because there's no telltale external cue that indicates something isn't true for you, but consider moments when . . .

- you go into a personal cliché, something you say often
- you feel like you need to justify something
- you lose contact with the sensations of your body

As for what you do write, truth can be a wide variety of things: *what year is this? what's your name? do you like your life? what do you need right now?* You could ask about something you're actually curious about. *What is this, really?* Or one of my favorites: *what do you know that you are trying to avoid knowing?*

Let the truth of these answers, what comes forth from pen to paper, surprise you.

* Thanks to Adyashanti for sharing this practice

ON CREATION

DUMB QUESTIONS

Dumb questions are the best questions. I've noticed that nearly any time someone says "I know this is a dumb question, but . . ." what comes out of their mouth next is asking about the fundamental nature of something. It's innocent and honest.

It's not a clever question. It's not "I understand all the rules and now I will ask about this particular facet of that understanding." Dumb questions say *wait, hold up . . . what are we doing here again?*

I can't think of more fertile grounds for creation than that. Consider making your own list of dumb questions before beginning a project, or when you feel stuck.

ON CREATION

ACTION

Love moves mountains, writes blog posts, and creates workshops, and it can do these things with clarity and urgency.

I slept and dreamt that life was joy.
I awoke and saw that life was service.
I acted and behold, service was joy.

— Rabindranath Tagore

STAYING MOTIVATED

You may ask yourself, as I have, how to stay motivated to work on your projects.

Consider how the question itself is already tilted in a certain direction. It assumes that what we really want to do is just kick it, perhaps sit on the couch and eat cupcakes all day. It assumes that we've got to stay motivated to do our work, otherwise our work won't happen.

Is this true?

Do you need to motivate yourself to listen to a song you love? I don't either.

It would be naïve to deny the utility of willpower, though I have noticed the clearer I am, the more honest I am with what I most love — and letting that knowing inform my every gesture and thought — the less there is to get motivated about.

We tend to motivate to follow someone else's rules. The energy to manifest the calling of your particular life may well need to be called something else.

BOLD ASSERTIONS

Make a bold assertion, something you feel but don't fully understand. Write yourself into a corner. Then look around.

Don't publish a bold assertion on its own merit; that's reckless. Don't say you're done until you really are, but also don't be afraid to not know what you're saying at first. Stay with it.

What called you here?

Some of my favorite chapters in this book began as baseless assertions. Many felt nauseating to me, watered-down spiritual truisms. Then I would panic. I would want to delete every word and forget it. Some I did delete, but many I stayed with, letting their nature reveal itself to me over time.

ON CREATION

NOT WRITING AS WRITING PRACTICE

The work of this book in its early stages — the first nine months, give or take — was mostly about not writing.

It was a lot of sitting down at a blank page with a pen, pausing and waiting at that precipice inside where I felt like something wanted to be said, yet whatever it was was still articulating itself in my psyche (or wherever all this stuff happens). It was burning, churning, still forming. *Don't turn away*, it said. *Stay here.*

I would spend minutes with my pen held to the page, feeling the forming and churning, not writing until the words made themselves known, easily and obviously. To do anything else, to either walk away or to write something insincere, would have been too painful.

Not doing — without disengaging — has been a tremendous practice for me.

SITTING QUIETLY

Consider spending a little time every day when you allow inspiration to come without trying to capture it.

Let your thoughts wander without pen and paper, without a phone, without even trying to remember what comes, even if it's a really good idea. All those mechanisms rest by the side for a minute; you just sit quietly.

It's like stepping out into a warm rain without trying to capture the droplets falling. That's not the good stuff. The sky cracking open is the good stuff, so behold.

ON CREATION

DESIRE

Desire is a main ingredient in the fuel for creation. It's also something many of us have a troubled relationship with, an uncomfortable fire we extinguish as soon as we can, either by getting what we want or by training ourselves not to want. This chapter is about the potential wisdom of the fire itself.

To desire, to want something, is to not have it. There's nothing wrong with this; anything under the sun moves towards what it's lacking.

When you were a baby who couldn't walk, eventually you figured it out — balancing on two feet, an impossibly complex task! — because you wanted to. We humans are phenomenally creative and resourceful in our movement towards our desires.

Desire breathes life into tired concepts. What might something like peace actually look like? You might find out if you want it badly enough. Not to say you'll then have it, but the wanting, the lack, is a void into which movement naturally flows. This is powerful unto itself, not merely as a means to attainment. Desire seeds the movement of creation.

ON DESIRE: A POEM

When you have a deep question,
one that sears your heart
with its why-ness,

what you really want
is relief from the burning.
And yet, every effort

to extinguish it is a
turning away. Why do this,
when you don't even know:

what is it?

PRACTICE: EMBODIED DESIRE THROUGH BREATH

Observe what's been happening your whole life: a breath born of desire. Your body craves an inhale when it's time, and moments later will crave an exhale. You don't need to think about either of those; it happens without thought.

If you're not sure what I mean, breathe all your air out, then don't breathe in until you feel the desire to. Anatomically, there are all sorts of chemical and mechanical receptors that guide this process. Experientially, it's much simpler: *I need this, now!*

Return to your regular breath. Notice the inhale and exhale are both born of your body's desire for the next thing. You're not wanting because you're incomplete or something is wrong. You're wanting because that's how breathing works.

THE ANATOMY OF DESIRE

In many traditions, the area of the body between the lower belly and sacrum is the font of creation. In Japanese healing arts this area is the *hara*; in Chinese medicine it's called the lower *dan tien*; in yoga the *svadisthana chakra*. Tending this area well and wisely is a cornerstone of these traditions.

This area is also the seat of our sexual organs: the uterus and ovaries, or prostate and spermatic cords (and where the testes reside for the first few months of life after birth, before descending).

For most of us, the lower-belly-to-lower-back area is immensely mysterious, and it's often difficult to feel anything at all there. It may be wise to offer a little loving attention now and then to such fertile grounds.

ON CREATION

PRACTICE: TENDING THE LOWER BELLY

Place one or both hands on your lower belly, between your belly button and your pubic bone. Now place your other hand, or imagine a hand that is warm and holding, on the lowest part of your lower back. If you're placing a hand here, you may feel the bony protrusions of the back of your pelvis. Your hands, real or imagined, are at the same latitude.

Feel into this area between your hands.

Notice your experience now, particularly bodily sensation. You have nowhere to go, either outwardly or inwardly. Just let your hands rest there, and listen with your whole body. (See "How to Listen to a Body" for a refresher.)

Breathe this way for a few minutes, then bring your hands together in front of your heart, and gently bow your head.

This may seem too simple to be of any use. Try it for seven minutes a day for twenty-eight days, and find out. Stay with the simplicity. Minds love complexity, which works wonders for building airplanes, but isn't the right tool for nurturing a relationship with the wilderness inside you.

PRACTICE: DESIRE AS FUEL

Consider feeling a desire arise and not acting on it one way or another as a potentially wonderful practice in the cultivation of your creative energy.

When the desire arises — to eat something sweet, have a drink, social media; the list of potential desires is endless — do two things.

> 1. See how it arose innocently. The wanting is independent of how you feel about it.

> 2. Bring your attention not to the object of desire, but to the bodily sensations of the desiring itself.

The aching in your chest, the heat in your face, the energy in your belly and genitals . . . whatever it is, experience that, for a breath or two, directly.

Don't think about it; do it.

I'd recommend to not make a plan about "whenever desire arises, I'm going to do this . . . " Just try it once. Notice if and how you feel enlivened by this practice, and try it again accordingly.

INFORMATION TOXICITY

As happened with food for much of the developed world, what was once scarce has become commonplace and all too easy to gorge on.

You may need more information for what you're working on. For many of us, though, the much more difficult and relevant invitation is to work more thoroughly and deeply with what you already know.

Consider keeping a small, hand-written note of information you need to look up. Once a day, look at that list and see what's still relevant, a burning question. Then go online, get your answers, and nothing more.

SELECTIVE HEARING

We are phenomenal at selective hearing. You were able to pick your mother's voice out of many long before you were able to form cohesive thoughts.

That you can only see part of a situation is not a defect. It is what gives you voice, context, and a relative viewpoint from which to create.

THREE KINDS OF MEDICINE

Note the times when you say "it sure is harder, if not impossible, to work on this project when I'm feeling this way" (tired, anxious, bereaved, etc). Given that ours is a process in which our creative projects are inseparable from the material of our lives, these difficulties arising should come as no surprise.

Consider three types of medicine for this predicament:

> 1. Direct. This is the archetypal father, "just keep going" approach. Do the work, despite what you feel, though also because of what you feel. Life doesn't stop at our whim. Keep going. Purification by fire. Keep going.

> 2. Indirect. This is the archetypal mother, "stop and tend to what's arising in you" approach. Drop the conflict by dropping the demands. You need time? Take time. You need rest? Then rest. Without guilt, without shame, lovingly hold any ache the best you can. Call a friend, take a walk. Give the hurt what it most needs, with care and without condition.

> 3. A third approach may arise without precedent. Without knowing if you will proceed with your work or not, turn towards the unsettling experience. Don't turn towards it because you think you should; only inquire if you are really curious: what is this that's arising? We know what it's called, but what, really, is it in your experience right now?

If this list resonates with you, you could bookmark this page. The next time something unpleasant enough to stop you in your tracks arises, contemplate each of the three approaches above and ask, "what would be most loving, useful, and kind here?"

You may get an answer, and that answer may guide you to keep going. Or it may prompt you to stop and tend to what's arising, call a friend, journal, or set up a session with your therapist. It may prompt you to do something you've never even thought about before.

How we are with whatever arises is a part of this practice of creation, as much as sitting down and working is.

CLICHÉ

Cliché is lazy and impotent use of language.

To say he is "as innocent as the day he was born" doesn't tell us much about this person's innocence at all. The words tend to fall flat. It's glossed over, not very vibrant. *Yup, got it. I already know this. Next.*

Just as important to remember is that clichés are cliché because they point to such common experiences.

This is really potent territory. We're someplace where a whole lot of people find themselves time and time again, but it's hidden by what we think we know.

When you find yourself writing in cliché, stop and appreciate this moment to take a fresh look, now. *What's it really like?*

This isn't about being clever, just accurate.

What do you see? What's it like, not in general, but in your direct experience, here and now?

> *A word is not a crystal, transparent and unchanged; it is the skin of a living thought and may vary greatly in color and content according to the circumstances and the time in which it is used.*
>
> — Oliver Wendell Holmes, Jr.

PERSONAL CLICHÉS

I'm generally less interested in the mantra you chant for an hour a day, and more interested in the mantras you say to yourself the other twenty-three.

— Gangaji

The most dangerous clichés are the ones we don't recognize as such, when they've been with us for so long, they're now a part of our perceptual bedrock. A personal cliché is an assumption about what something is. And that assumption, however true it has been, by its nature lacks intimacy and urgency.

We all have ideas that are more likely to be glossed over than others. Words like *success, failure, progress, winning, getting it right, love* and *hate, helping* and *hurting* . . . even close-to-the-skin ideas like *pleasure, pain, enjoyment,* and *disgust* . . . can be terrain we walked through long ago, and now don't even see. We're already looking for the next thing, because we think we already know this thing. That's the danger of cliché.

Pleasure, for example, can be very evocative. When we write or speak of pleasure, are we holding it safely at arms length? Or do we allow it to be loosened from its conceptual confines, and go deeply into our bodies where who knows what it will evoke?

That can be scary! It can also be enlivening and exhilarating.

I've noticed often, and perhaps paradoxically, the more passionate I am about an idea, the higher likelihood it is to become cliché for me, something I "believe in" but don't fully

ON CREATION

grock what I'm pointing to. Words like *insight, embodiment,* and *healing* point to this phenomenon in my journey.

Therein lies the paradox: I wasn't drawn to stop talking about those things because they were cliché to me. They were cliché to me because they were so important to me, so ubiquitous in my life.

Slowing down and feeling my way through ideas is a chance to get to know, again and anew, what I'm actually talking about.

It's like saying to the word-entities I love, "I'm sorry, I assumed I knew who you were through and through" and to inquire again into the nature of what I'm wanting to say.

If what I love changes, I want to support that. That's creation.

I heard a wonderful story of a poet who had been married for something like 50 years. When asked about his wife, he replied, "I know her so well at this point that she is a complete mystery to me."

PRACTICE: LIBERATING CLICHÉ

Let's pause for a moment to meditate not on what we consider to be special, but what we consider to be already known.

What are some words or ideas like that for you?

You might think about words you say or write about a lot. Perhaps it's part of your professional title, or your business name, or what you'd answer if someone asked "what's really important to you?"

Once you've got a word or two, this is not a time to berate them for being clichés. It's a time to hold them gently and sweetly, and let your genuine curiosity do the work of loving what they evoke in you. Remember, these words point to something important for you, and that's beautiful!

Look at them without assumption. This can be disorienting to any part of us that is afraid the world might fall apart without the energy that this word holds for us.

Love, for example. This is not deciding whether you like or don't like love, whether you need more or less of it, though all of that and more will affect your relationship with the word. You are just asking what energy for you, personally, is contained by the living skin of this word?

A few breaths of sincere attention on this can be plenty. Let it go at the first hint of boredom. Don't worry, what's real for you will keep finding you. Your deep psyche will work with this while you sleep.

EFFORT

The word *effort* is one I'd like to highlight as a personal cliché for many of us, especially as it applies to our work.

I've found through my own practice and conversations with others that *effort* is usually something we think is good and noble, or that it is the opposite of *ease* and thus a sign of misalignment. I'm not even sure what it means to me anymore, and that's the spirit I'd like to bring into this chapter.

Effort can point to so many different experiences: the effort of grinding a day-to-day job that you hate for 50 years is probably really different than the effort of a final sprint to kick the winning goal in a soccer game. Does it take effort to make love or dance tango? What about to make a speech when you're terrified? To speak your mind in the face of adversity?

Does it take effort to breathe? You could likely answer either way.

Is effort valiant, something you do for love and family? Is it something your partner or parents want you to exhibit more of? Is it an illusory byproduct of a separate self?

The question that stopped my gears turning was this: *Is trying hard actually more difficult than taking it easy?*

Let your deep-feeling bodymind do the investigation here. A little attention, and then letting it be a question for you to whatever extent you're actually curious about it, is plenty and has a wisdom of its own.

TRYING HARD

Oh, how much energy I've put into unimportant tasks in attempt to avoid facing my projects, heart-to-heart! It feels like I'm nervously pacing a room: checking email for the fifth time, writing a social media post for a little dose of attention, choosing the perfect photo for part of a class before I've gotten to the heart of what that section is even about. It's a lot of busy work to avoid the real work before me.

It's a feeling sense of being a little boy, trying to show mom and dad how hard I'm working, like I might catch a break if I looked pitiful enough. That way, if it doesn't work out, at least I tried hard. Everyone could see *that*. If I completed my work with perfect style, who would pity me then?

I don't think "well, just don't try so hard" is useful advice for many of us. The invitation is to follow this phenomenon to its roots.

PUTTING ON A GOOD SHOW

Trying hard as a waste of energy is well-demonstrated as a physical practice.

Imagine you're going to push a stone. The stone may be heavy but moving it is well within your capabilities. Imagine the show you could put on if you wanted to look like you were working really hard trying to move it, without actually moving it. You could grunt and strain, tense your muscles and even fully fatigue yourself without having actually done anything.

Were you working hard? Yes, undoubtedly.

Try it at a wall if you'd like. Push against the wall in a way where most of the tension remains in your body. Notice how different this is than pushing in a way where your force goes into the wall.

PRACTICE: DIALOGUE

"Who would I be if I wasn't trying hard?"

It's a question you might ask, quietly and with sincerity, if and when you notice you're busying yourself instead of engaging your real work.

Write the question down. Or sit in a chair and ask it aloud.

Then, see if a response comes to you on paper. Write it down. Or, if you said it aloud, get up and sit in another chair, listen to the question you'd asked moments before, and see if a reply comes. Speak that reply aloud.

Go back and forth between question and answer as much as feels fruitful. The most important thing here is the sincerity of the question, so take the time, energy, and your innate truth detection skills to find a question that feels genuinely exciting, perhaps uncomfortably so, for you.

PAYING ATTENTION IS PLAY

After all this talk of liberating cliché and following effort to its roots, let's orient to play as a fundamental process of creation. Play is spontaneous and fun. Humans, many animals, and perhaps even plants exhibit a kind of play.

For years I tried to pay attention to life's subtle unfoldings. "What's this *really* about?" I'd ask, furrow-browed. It was a discipline. That practice was wonderful as far as it went, but there was a tension inherent in my approach. I was trying to get it right, to remain vigilant and not make a mistake, and that was stressful. You, me, and any animal will lose its sense of play with enough stress.

You can't force play. You can't say, "alright, enough stressing out; stop that and play!"

But we can love it. We can feel a genuine longing to play, to participate in the improvised dance of living.

Is there not a bit of a game happening right now? With your breath and the air around you, with the sounds singing into your ears, with the objects you see, however dull and familiar, longing also to be seen, loved, danced with? The thoughts in your head, the echoes of memories past, the air on your skin ... do these all not riff off one another, mutually informing and co-creating this one experience you're having now?

That's play. And it's creation underway.

SIMPLE AND COMPLEX

Whether your project is "3-Minute Abs" or a unified theory to align general and quantum physics, you might ask yourself whether you consider what you're doing to be simple or complex.

Is there much energy around that for you? Perhaps pride or shame in your project's simplicity or complexity?

Consider how this practice we're engaged in is not defined by complexity. Its nature is neither verbose nor simple. Those are descriptors we apply after the work is done, looking in the rearview mirror at what just happened. They're not helpful predeterminates.

This practice asks only: what truly wants to be created here?

RESTRICTIONS

Because you don't have everything you want is why you are impelled to create.

Your body wouldn't create the movements of breathing if she didn't need to, the harmonious dance of too little and too much.

What you're going through, personally, in a time of creation are the spices that will make the dish delectable for someone else.

Bodily, restrictions are synonymous with shape and substance. No restrictions means no shape, means no movement.

Don't wait until there are no restrictions to engage with, nor to complete, your work. The restrictions are as much it as what flows through and around them.

LET IT BREATHE

Letting your project breathe on its own is an act of trust in an orchestrating intelligence.

There is no good reason anyone would believe that an embryo that has not drawn a single breath in its entire life to date should somehow know how to do that at just the critical moment after he is born. We wouldn't believe it if it didn't happen with such regularity.

So consider not what you want your project to be. What is your project already, and what is it asking for now? What is the feel of the divine breath happening here? What is that first, often-terrifying flash that you see before you start to make pro and con lists about where to go from here?

NO GUARANTEES

Remember, despite what you or I or anyone else thinks about what you're doing, there are no guarantees you're the right one for the job, that your work will be any good.

What a relief.

Listen to your intuition. Listen to other people. At the end of the day, there's really only one way to find out what your work will be like: do it.

DISORIENTATION

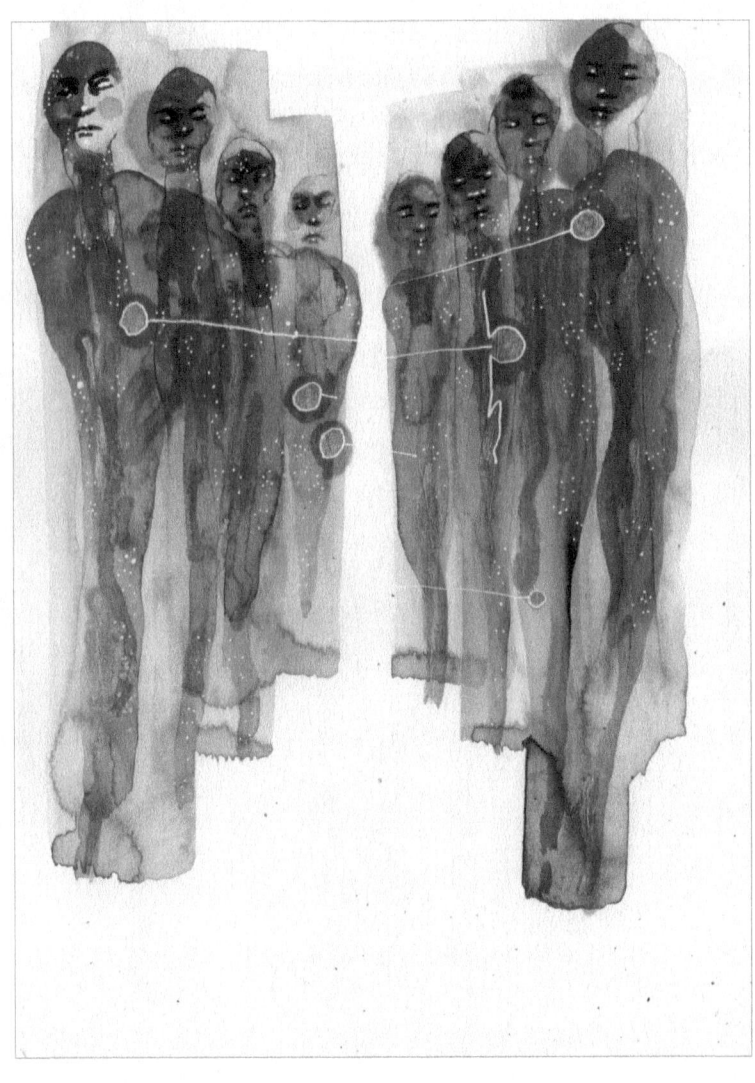

We delight in the beauty of the butterfly, but rarely admit the changes it has gone through to achieve that beauty.

— Maya Angelou

SHOCKED INTO DISORIENTATION

When your life falls apart, as it does, the surety of who you are and where you're going falls away.

(This surety is synonymous with cliché as we've been using it.)

I would never suggest pretending to enjoy suffering. This is only a reminder that some of your hidden gifts bloom in the fertile soil of disorientation.

When you're well oriented, you know what you know.

When you're disoriented, you don't know what's real, so you have to look — a most natural response, in an attempt to get oriented — but you can't rely on old ideas of what this is like, whatever *this* is. You have to look, as if for the first time, to find out.

FREE FALL

Imagine you are in a free fall. The ground is nowhere in sight; all you know is you are falling.

How much panic would naturally arise if you were trying to find out which way was up and which was down, to get your bearings in the way you're used to.

How much might you relax, and be able to sense more clearly, if you simply acknowledged the actual experience: you are in free fall and you don't know where you are in relation to any stationary body.

It still doesn't mean you know anything about anything.

It just means you are not freaking yourself out trying to get oriented.

VIA NEGATIVA

Some practices are defined by what they are not.

The via negativa, for example, is a theological approach that attempts to clarify what God is by addressing only what God is not.

The yogic practice of neti neti is another example, in which the practitioner looks at what arises in her consciousness and asks, "am I this?" The practice never poses its central question: *What am I?* The living-answer to this question reveals itself, over time, by experientially seeing what you are not.

I believe there's some of this pedagogy at work in this book. It relies on the magic of disorientation, rather than a class of sufficient orientation. It relies a lot on a particular person ready for a particular approach. May this find you well.

What's it like when you are sufficiently disoriented to see the world is not what you thought? It's not to say you know what the world is, but the questions you ask, and how you engage, are so vastly different than the moments when you thought you knew what the world was.

KNOWING OUR PROJECTS

We never fully know what our projects are until they are done, and when they're done they aren't our projects anymore.

DISORIENTATION

TERRIBLE FEELINGS

Engaging in this practice can evoke all sorts of godawful feelings. While creating, I have experienced plenty of . . .

- shame, like I was being caught in the middle of some terrible act

- feeling like a phony, about to be discovered

- feeling like a total loser, like for real, it's over for you, Bowler

. . . to name a few.

Try as I did to seek affirmation, no amount of anyone's words, even mine, could ever truly satisfy these primal uprisings.

"Well, look around. You're not doing anything bad; there's nothing to be ashamed of."

"Just keep going. Remember, this kind of thing happens."

"You're not a loser. You're a super guy."

While all of that is true, I always cringed a bit at summarizing difficulties with "this is normal and these feelings will pass; here's something nice to think about in the meantime."

I've begun to see these visiting feelings, the proverbial inner critic, in a different light, as a kind of litmus test for what I'm working on. They're saying "you'll never be enough." What would I feel compelled to do anyway, even if I were never enough? The critic-feelings are like microbes, digesting time and aspiration. What's left when you're out of time and hope?

They're saying, "hey, are you pretending anything here? Are you creating for some future time when you'll be vindicated? Do you know what you're saying in your bones, or are you posturing?"

This is not some reverse psychological trick to never have to experience a critical voice in your head again. It's about a relationship with whatever arises. In a moment of painful uprising, what else is there besides the direct experience? *I feel ashamed.* Innocently, that's true. I do feel that at that moment. There's nothing to argue with, and all that is arising is part of the creation process.

TURNING TOWARDS

Some of the most consistently surprising solutions in my life have appeared after turning towards difficult feelings. I know they're difficult because an inner voice says *oh no, not this again! If only this feeling weren't here, I would be creative and happy, like I was the other day.*

To turn towards a difficult feeling is one of the most challenging things I can think of to describe, even to myself. I have no plan or strategy on how to do it — or rather, I've had many such plans, but they never reliably pan out. It's like all words, all strategies, are already off the mark in that they divide reality by their nature, evoking directionality — *you're in a bad place, and this is about getting to the good place* — and the invitation is to stop going in any direction for a moment, to be taken under.

There are many myths in many cultures about the wisdom of being taken under, of the swamp, the shadow, the darkness. And they're all just words until you experience it, willingly or not. When you signed up to know your own authentic voice of creation, you signed up for this. I did, too. Let's turn towards our own blessed darkness authentically, alone, together.

DISORIENTATION

TURNING TOWARDS: A THOUGHT EXPERIMENT

Imagine you're practicing tai chi in your back yard. It's a daily practice you've engaged in for years, one you know and love deepening into. Some kids show up and point at you and laugh, saying "haha, you look silly!"

- You could get defensive: "Actually, kids, I'm practicing an ancient art that engages my kidney fire and chi! You idiots don't know what you're talking about. I am worthy!"

- You could hide inwardly, and pretend to ignore them. Say to yourself *they're just kids, I'm an adult. I'd better not lose my cool.*

- Or you could feel the flush of rage as it courses through your body. Feel the tears that long to be shed, the sadness of being called out. From this more embodied place, you might see their innocence in saying what they're saying, and how that has literally zero percent correlation to what tai chi is for you. You don't practice to impress kids; you practice for all it does for you.

You might laugh right along with them. "Looks funny, huh? Anyone want to join me?" What you actually do at that point doesn't really matter. What matters is that you're not making the kids out to be idiots for seeing what they see, or yourself an idiot for loving what you love, and doing what you do.

Maybe some change comes from acknowledging the terrible feelings that arise while you're working; maybe not. What's important is how you stand all the while. Willingness, humility, and experience will do the rest.

DISORIENTATION

SLOWING DOWN AND DECOUPLING

Disorientation has a way of slowing us down, does it not?

The kind of slowing down I'm hoping this book will foster doesn't ultimately have to do with speed in any traditional sense. It's more like a kind of disentangling, of allowing constituent parts to be sensed by your innate intelligence.

In this sense, "slow down" points in the same direction as "notice" or "pay attention."

This practice of decoupling movements is a centerpiece in many body-centered methods. The one I am most familiar with is the work of Moshé Feldenkrais. The central idea is that we feel pain and are stiff because we work too hard to do most everything.

Imagine tensing all your muscles when you go to pick up a glass of water: butt squeezed, face scrunched, full body flexing. A very small portion of that tension, hidden in a sea of extraneous tension, is necessary to do the action.

By slowing down the movement and paying attention to what happens, we create more space to feel into these conditioned patterns. The awareness itself reorganizes the body around this new seeing, dropping some of the superfluous effort. One of the hallmarks of a seasoned practitioner is how they move with a kind of beautiful efficiency, no matter the task.

The work isn't slow so that you move slowly through life. The slowing down is a method to hear each note

of the chord, each piece of the quick succession of movements that culminate in one big movement. And then, via the body's ability to spontaneously recalibrate, a note that may have been a little flat or sharp comes into tune, into better relation with the other notes.

May this book also encourage slowing down, not to try to make an army of glassy-eyed, syrupy-slow people who pretend everything is fine. Our aim is to disentangle and let breathe the *prima materia* of our experiences, so that when we get back to it after some slowing down, some intricate paying attention, our way of working is somehow, almost magically, more easeful than it was before.

THE PERIPHERY

We often speak about the periphery as having meaning only when it is a field we are moving out of, and into focus.

Perhaps periphery has a meaning and intelligence of its own.

Bodily, peripheral seeing is a different phenomenon than focused seeing. For example, you don't sense a moving object as well when you're focusing on it; movement is much more keenly detected in the periphery.

Metaphorically, periphery could point to that which you can sort of know, but also can't articulate. It could be a sense of being a little fuzzy-headed about something. A common reaction would be to try to be less fuzzy-headed, to get more focused and clear. But perhaps your peripheral sensing is the best tool for that particular body of work right now. Maybe the heart of what you're working on is still forming, and would wither and die in the direct sunlight of focus, so despite your best efforts, your deep wisdom keeps it in the shadows.

You don't dig up seeds to make sure they're still in the soil. You nurture them, and let them do their seed thing until they're ready to bloom, to come into vision.

Consider that what's in your periphery is just fine there. Just because it's not in focus doesn't mean you can't see it perfectly.

ANTIFRAGILE

Your bodymind thrives to a certain extent on things not going according to plan, to conditions not being perfect.

We once marveled at how technology would help us take out all the bad stuff in life, and keep only the good stuff. Of course, it's not really panning out like that.

> Ditch the bran and germ of a grain; they don't seem to be doing much anyway.
>
>> *Oops, nevermind. Fiber is important.*
>
> Sanitize every surface and make your home germ-free.
>
>> *Oops, nevermind. Those germs are an essential part of developing our immune systems.*
>
> Support your arches with these high-tech, super cushioned shoes.
>
>> *Oops, nevermind. Our feet thrive on contact with the ground, and arches are elastic structures that don't develop as well if they're supported from underneath.*

This is not to say the more hardship, the better. That's silly. It is to speak to the deep care potential within the stressors of disorientation. Your palate knows this: eating only saccharine-sweet gumdrops will make you sick.

It can be quite disorienting to see how our quests for comfort are killing us, as they have been killing others for a long time.

> Your most important work may feel troubling at first.

DISORIENTATION

BURN EVERYTHING YOU'VE EVER DONE

Consider burning all your old notebooks (or recycle them for the same outcome with a less dramatic flair).

Delete all the "someday I'll get to this . . ." projects on your computer. All your good ideas, all your bad ideas, everything you're not actively working with. Don't go through them one last time. They're gone.

Then stand back. You have nothing to remember. What's left?

DISORIENTATION

WHAT REMAINS?

Consider letting your best self have a rest today.

Those wonderful, have-it-all-together characters we can sometimes muster up — often with a strong cup of something caffeinated — but who go all too quickly . . . let them rest.

There's a question you may have skipped over: what is it to create from your average self, the ordinary one who isn't very exciting? What might they have to say if we don't rush them, or pressure them to be special?

This is one of the simplest and most terrifying practices I know. Yet every time I've been stripped naked through defeat, my best self face down on the floor in exhaustion, I have been surprised by what was still here, seemingly of its own accord.

Let your best self rest. What remains?

The opposite of faith is not doubt, but certainty.

— Anne Lamott

TOWARDS COMPLETION

SOME QUESTIONS YOU COULD ASK YOURSELF AT THIS POINT

How will I know when this project is finished?

How much longer will this take? Am I sure of that?

If I only had one day left to complete this project, what would I do? What if I had 100 more years?

What would this look like if it were easier?

Are there any bits of stone, however beautiful, that I might remove to allow the inner form of this project to articulate itself more clearly?

Is there anything here that's trying to win an argument, that's trying to prove a point in a way that doesn't serve the gift that wants to come through?

COMPLETION

To say "I am done with this" can be equally relieving and panic inducing. It could always be better, and your reflection on your work will be different in ten years, perhaps even in ten minutes.

Any parent knows this dilemma well: when and how to hold and defend your children, and when and how to let them be in the world on their own two feet. This process with my own son has broken my heart 10,000 times and counting, wanting so passionately for him to experience nothing but the finest, and the gut-rendering realization that the finest also includes stepping forward into unknown territory, a breath of wind on his face, his own feet on the ground.

To complete a project is to allow its birth. It doesn't mean you stop caring or that you couldn't work on it forever. It just means it's ready to be on its own two feet out there.

COMPLETION AND SAYING NO

To offer a container for an infinitely wild energy to take a particular form in can be a gift, and it's as much about "no" as it is "yes."

In general . . .

> To say no to an invitation can be to say yes to what you're doing now.
>
> To offer few options can be a gift to someone overwhelmed by choosing.
>
> To not know something is to be in relationship with it.

And specifically about our work . . .

> To not solicit feedback about a project at this stage can be to tend its forming with care.
>
> To complete a project is by its nature to offer something incomplete, because if it's something, it's not everything.
>
> To limit your project to a certain form is a practice unto itself.

TOWARDS COMPLETION

LAST-MINUTE ADDITIONS

Beware of major additions near the end of a project.

This is not to say don't do it, but consider stopping when you feel the impulse to just squeeze one last little gem of an idea into your project, even if it doesn't quite fit.

Stop and let it rest. Move on for a bit.

If you return to the idea and it fits this project, by all means add it.

Otherwise, perhaps it's your next project saying hello.

THE LAST TWO PERCENT

I have rushed through the final touches, the last two percent, of hundreds of projects. All my energy was with it until it was almost over, and then suddenly I couldn't even bear to think about it. I just wanted to be done; *get me out of here and onto the next thing!*

I would teach the class without one or two final read-throughs of my notes. I would press "publish" on a piece that was almost crafted, but not quite. In every instance, I squirmed, and tried to get away from a certain aspect of myself that was emerging at this stage of the practice.

This is prime material to work with. Those projects I rushed the completion of turned out fine — it's not like they were worthless — but that's not the point. I've been surprised by all that is embedded in that burning hot coal called "finishing well." It's like its own little world.

Avoiding it and rushing the end won't kill you, but I've found it wise to use a little willpower, to step back and pause when I feel the urgency arise of needing to be done, now.

What does that urgency actually feel like? We know what it's saying, but what is the direct experience of the urgency itself?

It might feel like you're going to die. And you are, but probably not because of this.

Finishing well can be a practice unto itself.

ON SHARING

I'd love to share these words of Jesus as recorded in the Gospel of Thomas:

> *If you bring forth what is within you,*
> *what you bring forth will save you.*
>
> *If you do not bring forth what is within you,*
> *what you do not bring forth will destroy you.*

What is within you is not relevant here. What's relevant is that you, and I, bring that forth.

I have no idea whether you should share your work, or how widely. How could I? We might ask simply what is being called for. What does bringing *this* forth look like? Make no assumptions.

VULNERABLE

It can feel vulnerable to share your work. You might get hurt.

Consider tending wisely the softness of your heart. Don't listen to anyone who critiques your work solely to make you feel bad.

But also remember: not sharing your work can hurt, too.

AFFECTED

To share your work is to be affected by the response.

It's part of the process, not a defect, that praise feels good and being ignored hurts. Poet David Whyte wrote,

We shape our self
to fit this world

and by the world
are shaped again.

That my posture and my work — both shape expressions — are embedded with longing is as natural as a plant yearning for the sun.

There is not *only* longing, but there is longing. I am affected by you.

PRACTICE: RELEASING AND RECEIVING

Completing a project is a releasing and a receiving. This practice is one way to attune to those energies.

Take a few breaths to orient to where you are. Settle into a comfortable seat. Say out loud, "I am beginning this practice." Bring your attention to your right hand, and your left hand.

On your next exhale, imagine releasing any extraneous tension from your whole body through your right hand. Don't overthink it, just give it a go for a few breaths.

Relax for a few breaths, being as kindly allowing as you can with whatever sensation arises.

On a following inhale, imagine receiving something wonderful with your left hand: an energetic gift, a warmth, a kindness, a generosity. You receive through your left hand and into your whole body.

Relax for a few breaths, being as kindly allowing as you can with whatever sensation arises.

Was one of those easier for you, the releasing or the receiving?

Say out loud, "this practice is now over" and be done with it.

Feel free to switch up your hands. In many traditions, the left side of the body is the yin, receiving side, and the right is the yang, arising side, though I think it's great to buck tradition to find out for ourselves what's true.

COMPOST

Remember this natural cycle: today's flower is food for tomorrow's flower. There's no other way.

This truth can seem sad and even vicious if we consider the two flowers to be completely different, unrelated entities. One dies so that the other may live. How different these same truths appear if we sense the underlying intelligence giving rise to the soil, the flowering, and the composting.

We need not choose one over the other. Grieve when your heart grieves. Also, rest on the earth. Our creations and, yes, our very own bodies express this living and dying.

TOWARDS COMPLETION

IMPACT

You'll never know the full impact of your work. Ever.

How many times have you picked up a book you were given years ago to find it was the perfect time to read it? How many tiny, forgettable moments from your childhood made you who you are today?

You never know who you'll affect, and how you'll affect them.

It's far too much to try to keep track of, so listen now to that quiet hum in your bones, that direct sensory experience of what now is. Listen to that with all of your heart, act from that place with full faith, and don't worry about your impact because you'll never know.

LETTING GO

To find out what your project is, let it go.

TOWARDS COMPLETION

AND NOW WHAT?

Your project is complete. You pressed "publish" on the blog post. Your book is printed and ready to order. Your art exhibit hung and is now taken down.

What now?

Consider how any premeditated answer falls more flat than what spontaneously arises within you.

Whether you take time off, or jump right into your next project, or something else, we can never know for sure what will be called for, can we? We're left with what we've had all along in this creation process: listen and respond, in succession and together at once.

TOWARDS COMPLETION

AFTERWORD

This book has been a magnificent gift to write. And I am thoroughly worked over from it. I feel like the writing was always a few steps ahead of me, and brought disorienting levels of honesty, clarity, and integrity to the forefront of my life.

We are in such a wild, difficult, unprecedented time as of this writing, too. My sense is we must learn to be more kind to each other if we are to survive. This is a deep, often terrifying project, to really open our hearts to one another, even and especially when we are emotionally triggered, or strongly disagree.

The open heart is so often confused with a lack of discernment, but I think a lot of us are seeing through that duality, too. Opening your heart isn't dopey; it's a radical, earth-shattering act. It's not bravado; it's surrender.

So many familiar constructs about who I was and where I was going have been dashed over the years. It's been incredibly liberating, on a personal level, and humbling in ways I couldn't have imagined. Everywhere I look, there I am. Our jails, mental health hospitals, abusers and victims alike, are all full of situations I could so easily be in. It is not by some wonderful central core of my being that I live in a nice place. I could be anyone under different circumstances.

Kahlil Gibran described love,

> *Like sheaves of corn he gathers you unto himself.*
> *He threshes you to make you naked.*
> *He sifts you to free you from your husks.*
> *He grinds you to whiteness.*
> *He kneads you until you are pliant;*
> *And then he assigns you to his sacred fire,*
> *that you may become sacred bread for God's sacred feast.*

Here's to it, fire and all. May we be worthy of love directing our course. May we take good care of each other, especially those enduring hardship. Life can be immensely difficult.

Love, Liam
Bellingham, WA

GRATITUDE

Jennifer, your experience, attentive mind, and caring heart brought this project from a smattering of writings to a cohesive experience. It's been a very meaningful journey for me to collaborate with you. Thank you for saying yes to this project.

Meg, your art practice has been an inspiration to me for years. It was a joy to get to join your work with this writing.

Danny, I feel so resonant with your music and general artistic aesthetic. I am so glad to have your touch as part of this book! Your work ethic was over the top, too.

To my parents — Mom and Bill, Pop and Kim — and my brother, Barley Zarathustra. I love you. Thank you for all that was involved in helping me find my way in the world in my young years, and beyond.

Thank you Master John Paul Noyes and Big Sky Martial Arts in Kalispell, Montana, for my first gig as a teacher, and for your fierce confidence in me as a young man.

Thanks Steven Pressfield, whose book *The War of Art* was a big influence on this book's voice and structure.

Thank you Matt Licata, whose immensely kind teaching I was immersed in during much of this writing.

Amy, your presence in my life has brought forth prayers I uttered millennia ago, out of the most unseen of my depths. You've shaped this book, and continue to shape the blossoming of what I used to think I understood, just by being you.

And Jonah, my wondrous son . . . Your arrival onto this planet has ushered my heart beyond the confines of my chest in a way I don't think I could ever describe. I love you immeasurably and am so, so, so, so, so glad you are here.

ABOUT THE ARTIST
Meg Yates

I love to paint! It's a joy to witness my inner life translate to outer expression through the process. The works selected for this collaboration are from my daily painting practice, a homecoming discipline I've been at for six years now. In addition to painting, I teach art, companion folks 1:1 and facilitate community circle gatherings.

For more about my art, classes and offerings, you can find me at:
www.meghan-yates.com

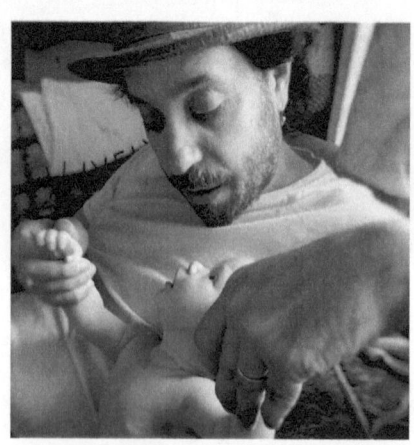

ABOUT THE DESIGNER
Danny Schmidt

I'm a full-time touring songwriter and performer. As such, there's nothing more purely fun than creating something outside my field of expertise. Helping Liam to shape his beautiful words and ideas into a correspondingly beautiful visual form has been a delightful return to creativity for its own sake.

For more about my music, I invite you to visit:
www.dannyschmidt.com

ABOUT THE EDITOR
Jennifer Sanders

As a lover of books and the written word, I cherish my role as editor of this book and other projects. I also support others working towards optimal health as a certified functional medicine health coach and yoga teacher. Beyond this work, I enjoy foraging in the wild woods to make plant-based medicine and reading at the roots of towering firs in the Pacific Northwest.

For more about my work, please write to me directly at:
functionalhealthcoach@gmail.com

ABOUT THE AUTHOR
Liam Bowler

This is my first book. I fell in love with the process and have already begun writing another. I host a podcast called *The Body Awake,* which is currently pretty dormant but may wake again, in one form or another. Find it, and other things I've created, including music and online classes, at: www.thebodyawake.com.

And please drop me a line to say hello if you'd like:
liam@thebodyawake.com

To purchase copies of this book
directly from the author, please visit:

thebodyawake.com/book/cc

www.ingramcontent.com/pod-product-compliance
Lightning Source LLC
Chambersburg PA
CBHW032039200426
43209CB00049B/29